In Badoc
and other poems

In Badock's Wood and Other Poems
Copyright © 2016 Mark Hamilton
Published by daisyPress

ISBN 978-1-910358-08-5

A catalogue record for this book is available from the British Library.

Cover image and design by Ian Young
With thanks to proofreader Meg Humphries

daisyPress is the fiction imprint of Daisypress Ltd
Bristol
England

daisypress.pub

In Badock's Wood
and other poems

By

Mark Hamilton

daisyPress

By the same author

The Arsenal and Other Poems
Love and Other Colours

Contents

... and other poems

Foreword

Badock's Wood is a beautiful and relatively little known area of woodland in north Bristol. I began walking my dog there regularly towards the end of 2014 and, inspired by the beauty and tranquillity of the place, wrote a poem about it.

One poem became two, and I began to think about writing a series of poems. Investigating the woods further, I realised there is a treasure trove of different aspects: a Bronze Age burial mound within the confines, a statue inscribed with a beautiful poem, a series of carved wooden benches, and a carving in a tree of the mythical wood spirit, the 'Green Man'. The origins of what we know today as Badock's Wood are fascinating too – the area being donated to the City of Bristol in 1937 by industrialist, philanthropist and Pro-Chancellor of Bristol University, Sir Stanley Badock.

The woods are also interesting because they sit in the middle of quite contrasting suburbs of the city. *In Badock's Wood and Other Poems* is, therefore, not only a collection of poems inspired by nature, but also by themes of history, time, social issues and the interplay of our emotions with the physical world.

For the curious, there is lots of information about the woods on the Friends of Badock's Wood website – www.fobw.org.uk – including the archaeology and history of the area and the flora, fauna and wildlife that can be found.

However, you don't need to know Badock's Wood to enjoy the poems. Nature is universal after all.

There are sixteen poems about Badock's Wood, which I have supplemented with sixteen other poems that share, in some way, a related theme: the natural world, the seasons, the passing of time, the spiritual sense, love.

I hope you will enjoy the poems, and perhaps go and seek out some woodland!

Mark Hamilton
June 2016
Twitter: @mhamilton1509

"Yet it creates, transcending these,
Far other worlds, and other seas;
Annihilating all that's made
To a green thought in a green shade."

Andrew Marvell, *The Garden*

For my wife Selda, and our dog Alfie

In Badock's Wood ...

In Badock's Wood

The simple pleasure
of a walk
through the wood,
always fresh
and leafmeal good,
under the wavering branches
that hold magpies and crows
and finches,
and quick squirrels like
grey squiggles
scampering up and down,
should be
repeated,
step by step along
the rain–bright path,
endlessly

Rainwalk

Taking the dog for a walk in Badock's Wood,
the clouds suddenly closed in
and a trouncing rain swept down on us
through the bare unsheltering trees.
Caught short, we were bedraggled,
nose-dripping, sopping and raw
of hand and paw, as we rounded
the corner and ascended
the path to the top.
But then the rain stopped
like a tap turned off,
a back-filling hush descended
— all was suspended —
and the sun broke through the cloud
like a stubborn guest.
We heard children in the playground
at break time, their shouts and laughter
ringing round the trees,
young excitement as it has always been,
as it was when I was a child,
unchanged, unchangeable,
and I looked at Alfie,
still dripping, rootling in the brambles,
and smiled.

Sir Stanley Badock

After the painting of Sir Stanley Badock by Herbert Gunn, which hangs
at Bristol University.

That's Sir Stanley Badock painted on the wall;
Can't tell much about him – looks quite inscrutable.
One leg thrown across the other, in his flowing gown,
Seems at ease within himself, the master of the town.
Is that a smile perhaps, hovering round his lips?
A playful ironist savouring wry and subtle quips?
Still, his air's patrician, commander of the scene,
Probably wouldn't suffer fools or anything in between.
(I'm attempting to ignore the thought – plainly barmy –
That he somewhat resembles Private Frazer of Dad's Army!)

His career, though, was serious, full of gravitas and weight
As he steered Bristol University, helped to make it great;
Started an industrialist, built his wealth on steel,
Then perhaps as assets grew, slowly came to feel
He should put something back, give something to the city,
Channelled his attention away from mere prosperity
To learning, knowledge's pursuit and wider social purpose –
Founded, indeed, Bristol's CIVIC LEAGUE OF SOCIAL SERVICE!

But was he a *good* man? How'd he treat family, juniors, servants?
Was he true not only in word but also in observance?
What did he believe, was he harsh, strait-laced, severe,
Or was he tolerant and flexible, a progressive pioneer?
The inner man's elusive; we can only look at what's behind
If we're to unravel the nature of his mind ...

It seems a simple thing, then, to judge if he was good!
For all around us lies his legacy – Badock's Wood.
These woods and fields, these meadows, a gift to the city,
A green and natural space, to remain in perpetuity.
One can only guess he loved it here, to walk from his grounds
By the trees and the river, stroll his quiet rounds.
So his mark, his monument, lies not in wealth or commerce,
Not in institutions' pillars or his own or public purse,
But in *this* place, where nature breathes, day by day, year by year:
Sir Stanley Badock's epitaph is greenly grounded, here.

Barrow

A little rise, a lump with two humps
— you can walk right past without
even noticing it's there.

But the silver statue beside it
is an enigmatic marker,
inscribed with its beautiful verse:
the curious walker will discover
that this tumulus is in fact
an ancient burial mound,
the 'Southmead Round Barrow',
three thousand years old or
Christ plus half again!

What bones, what flints of women, men,
lie inside it, mingled with old earth
and stone? So old they're beyond
ageing; so long gone they might never
have been. But they were *here*,
they stalked across these meadows
and fields, their blood and bone drama
everything that was. And they are marked
and remembered by the metalled
menhir that stands and makes a prism
from the sun. That has been done.

It is for us as we pass, thinking
of what we're doing today or tomorrow,
what email or text has just come,
to stop and look and see;
to mark the marker
so that life, in its fragments,
may minutely have won.

Ghostly sails

In tribute to the poem by John Fairfax and the monument
created by Michael Fairfax, his son, in Badock's Wood.

A wonderful whorl of words,
a circle coming round on itself
even as it progresses back —
back in time with the ghostly
windmill sails that turned
on Milltut Field, back further still
to bronze age warrior whose
burial place was here, while wolves
prowled and deer nervously grazed ...

The vivid lines leave their mark,
scored on the monument
that stands in ageless guard:
crossing the meadow,
the sails turn invisibly in the mind
while wild men and women
dart like shadows between the trees.

The original poem by John Fairfax, which is laid out on the monument
in a curled pattern, is reproduced below.

At Badock's Wood ghostly windmill sails turn
and like a rewound film spin through history
to remote times when this mound was burial
for bronze age warrior.
In that past landscape wolves prowled
and nervy deer grazed
while wild hog rooted among trees.

Climate unchange

What would our Bronze Age brothers
and sisters hunting in Badock's Wood
have made of this?
Spring peeping out in January,
summers wet and wild,
autumns long and honeyed,
winters late and mild?
Ah, they wouldn't have blinked,
would have pierced the quietly grazing deer
with their black, black eyes
as they pulled back the bowstring
and fired ...

Burn out

Burnt scooter in the middle of the field.

Charred and twisted;
angry at its fate.

It seems naked, stripped bare
as it sits there, urban scarecrow,
in a pool of grey–black ash.

Kids.

Bored of course, nothing
to fucking do on the estate
in the empty holidays.

Now and again they nick a bike,
ride it up round the woods
and set it alight:
modern sacrifice, burning
lousy altar.

Within a few days it's gone.
Don't know who took it —
the moped social workers?

The burnt grass heals itself in time.
A month later there's no sign
it was ever there — the green
has a smooth sheen, the crows
cross it unperturbed.

So nature renews itself.

The kids will take longer to heal
though,
circling the barren streets
looking for more time to kill.

Entries

Tardis-type trick at Badock's Wood:
entries the same, exits not.
Take which entry you will,
it is the same green
continuous world breathing
out its freshness.
But exits bring you
various: Tudor beams, trim hedges,
cars puffed on the drive;
or, on the other side,
tough squat streets, pitted
and patched, subsisting.
Nature is seamless;
world is fractured,
split by circumstance.
The green wavering rises,
lovely vision
wherever viewed.
But its equal, unpriced promise
remains unreachable,
yet or ever.

Match of the day

A deep roar rumbles down the hedgerow
in the afternoon gloom:
the rugby match is nearing its end.
The swell of noise seems to come
under the hedge, not over −
earthy, made of mud and blood and bone.

"Come on lads, get stuck in!
Fucking give it everything in the last ten!"

So the local rivals fight it out,
a smattering of spectators urging them on.
On this side the hedge, Badock's side,
there's football sometimes (never the twain shall meet).
Same story − clattering tackles, curses and cheers,
celebration as though life depended.
No matter the crowd is a dozen,
no matter the pitch is a slope with no nets.
The contest's the thing, the pride
of it. The personal achieve too,
the flashes of skill, the sudden elegance
conjured like a plate spun, no hands,
by the would−be should−be stars!

They have the tics of the pros to boot —
the flicks and kicks, the jinks and feints,
the innocent-face appeals to the ref.
Though those glowing pros are worlds away
with their stadia and their lights, the wages
as big as a mortgage every week.

But who's imitating who?
A reverse pass in the fading light
sets the wing haring for the line
and suddenly it is the stars
who are chasing the dream,
trying to get back to where it all began,
where everything is just as it is,
and the game will end with three cheers
and a bevy of beers down the pub.

Roots

The maples on the meadow's edge
may be slender.

But they're strong.

Their long, bony fingers
push up through the path,
a criss-cross of slow
violent ridges that
concrete can barely contain.

Call it crazy paving,
call it the horror
of something beneath the surface
that refuses to die.

The roots will not be denied.

Nature is as hard as nails,
let man bang at it
as he will.

So the wind will blow,
and the rain will rain.

The wind blows coldly through me
as I step along the path.

Visions of paper swirling,
bills, must–do's, demands.

Life is as hard as nails,
nothing will be damn well denied.

Remittance

That moment
a payment advice arrived,
blinking on my phone
as dusk was falling
deep beneath the trees,
late one Friday afternoon
in Badock's Wood,
and there would be money
to wriggle through with
after all.
That!

The dogs and hounds of Badock's Wood

The dogs and hounds
Of Badock's Wood
Make a motley crew,
As they should!

There's retriever, pug,
Alsatian and poodle,
And cocker–cava–
Labra–doodle.

My favourite though's
My own chihuahua
Who scampers round
And makes *brouhaha*!

Their tails wagging,
Their eyes all bright,
They run and chase
In dog–delight.

They greet with
Canine etiquette,
Though what that is
I've not figured yet.

It's not quite clear
What they follow,
Who sniffs first
In which dog-hollow!

We could learn though
From their furry mores —
Direct and true,
No subtle scores.

They keep us young,
They keep us active;
They help us be
More interactive:

They break the ice,
Help humans talk
When they take us
For a walk!

All hail the dogs
Of Badock's Wood;
Make a motley crew,
As they should!

Greengages

Briefly, I wished your name was Anne!

Then I could have called you
Anne of Green Gages
as you plucked them from the branches
that soft and sunny afternoon
by the field in Badock's Wood,
and the hard, sharp fruit
caused little explosions in our mouths.

Such is nature's bounty —
free to air (and wind, and rain),
free to those who stop
to take its miracle work
in glad and grateful fingers.

New & improved

"Dear valued customer,
Have we got news for you!
We are continuously listening
To customer feedback and researching
Ways to make our products
Even better! And so, we're delighted
To announce
That we are launching a new & improved
Ash tree! It will be 25% smaller
So as to be more manageable
Around the home; we're making
The bark smoother for a richer, creamier
Finish;
We're giving the leaves a more durable,
Polished sheen;
And redesigning the branch distribution
Into a more optimal format
So the little ones can climb and play
On it with greater ease (though, of course, we're
Retaining all the safety features
That have made us the market leader
For the past ten years, voted number one
In 'Your Ash Tree Provider' three years consecutively now*).
We're delighted to offer you an introductory discount
Of 25% on orders placed before the end
Of this month — so hurry, as must end soon!

*Three consecutive years except for the middle one, when ranked second.

Based on *your* feedback,
We're also relaunching the tree under a NEW BRAND!
It will in future be known as the *Flash tree*™!
'Ash' tree having negative connotations, rightly
Or wrongly, of cancer and death.
We think *Flash tree*™, with its suggestion of
Happening and excitement, is uniquely
In line with the
Values and aspirations that power
Our Brand.
It's all part of the way we're continually striving
To improve our service to you – and
Contact you to generate
More sales!
Just quote the code 'Flashcrap' against
Your next purchase, in-store or online,
To receive your discount.
We're delighted to have you
As a valued customer and hope
That you'll be spending more money
With us soon.
Credit's available too – to a pretty tune!"

Meanwhile, in the woods, dawn turned
To midday turned to afternoon;
The crows cawed, the finches flitted,
And the ash trees quietly stretched themselves
In the breeze.

Ash from elder

Is that beech or chestnut?
Hazel or hawthorn, that?
And may that be ... a wood anemone?
Don't ask me –
I suffer from natural illiteracy.

I don't know my ash from my elder ...

Difficult to learn, hard to self-teach,
does it matter?
A tree's a tree and a shrub's a shrub,
call them what you will.

So I wander round and enjoy the scene
in all my hairy ignorance:
return to a primitive state.

Though still, I have my phone
and can tweet from
among the trees.
I tweet there like a bird ...

Is that a wren, a wagtail,
a dunnock, a tit?
Who knows it?
I don't.

But the beauty's the same
as it lifts its wings
and sweeps along the river's course ...

That's why we come.

Don't know the names —
it's a fog, a haze, even with
my glasses on.

But whatever it's called,
whatever properties it has,
it's green thoughts, green shade:
that green, deep-running jazz.

All the world

If all the world was Badock's Wood
— all would be well and good.
There's woodland, meadow, mound, and field
And paths both down and up.
So many trees you cannot see,
Wildflowers and moss and fern;
Birds of all feathers,
Creatures for all weathers,
And rivers gurgling through.
There's a place to live, what's more,
In the bamboo by the 'fall;
Not waterproof, it's true,
But green and natural!
There are places to sit
Carved from trees,
And a green man down
In the corner; his spirit
Hovers and breathes through
The woods — it's spooky
At dusk I warn yer!

I'd live here if I could,
Despite the fact I can't.
There's everything and more you need
If you could live on flower and plant.

... and other poems

Creation

On the first day God woke up.

On the second day he yawned,
stretched like a light

right across the third.

On day four he was still,
let himself fill
all the space he was in …

It was on the fifth day
that he suddenly remembered:
"Oh my God!" he thought, "I nearly forgot!
I knew there was something!"

Day six was incredible.
He made a whole world,
in one lightning swirl
of creative genius.

It was remarkable:
no one else could have done it.

It was so beautiful, God could have cried.

Then on the seventh day
he cried.

Because, having worked at such brilliant pace,
he saw there were flaws
amidst the perfection:
little cracks that would open
over time and be the cause
of endless grief.
The little mirrors of himself
contained the largest cracks,
from side to side,
though still they dazzled,
like points of the sun.

Once created, things could not be undone,
not even by God.

He trembled with helpless love for it,
and glittered from the tears in his eyes.

Bishop's Stortford, Herts

One dark Sunday afternoon in January,
trailing back from KFC to the car,
past half-hearted shops half empty
with shoppers like shadows, half-spent,

the children, my wife and I,

were stopped, astonished,
by a crowd of dim birds
in a clump of thin trees
singing like a mad choir of angels

– there in Bishop's Stortford, Herts –

rapt in a ravishing realm of their own,
trilling, spilling, billowing out joy
for no reason except they were alive

(no sunset, no sunrise, no light breaking
in celestial skies),

just singing,
on a dull grey afternoon,

because they were alive, alive,
because *that* is the important, the
magical thing,

because life, no matter what, life,
as soon as it stops,

starts

Moonshine

Unable to sleep, I slip out for a fag
at 3 a.m. – and am amazed
by the moon, hanging
like a burnished half-shield
in the field of night around it,
a noiseless trumpet-blaze
of light in the pin-pricked black
that stretches above me, back.

An unseen glory while the city sleeps,
what is it for? It seems to say something,
to signify more …

But I suppose it doesn't.
It is beautiful, a vivid shock,
a flash, a cosmic splash, like …

No, it's beautiful, that's all.

It is one of the hardest things to do,
the loneliest,
to let go of good old
pathetic fallacy.

Still, I take it with me back to bed
and as I lay my head
it is shining hazily inside, a night light
fading with me to sleep.

Transmutation

This coffee is like a miracle:
oil-slick black,
thick as night,
a transmutation of water
which has journeyed through
deep earth
to emerge, by a secret
ministry,
worlds different from before.

Water has lifted out the spirit
of the grounds.
They brood together now,
darkly locked,
held by a spell that cannot
be reversed.

I drink:
its force is a kick,
a slap of the sea
in a cave,
lapping its secrets of ocean.

I wreathe it round with the burning
of tobacco:
leaf turns to flame turns
to smoke,
rising like an offering,
winnowing
up ...

It stirs in me – like crystals of sugar
revolving, dissolving –
a cry for transmutation.

My body and my mind are soothed,
are roused – strangely both –
but what can reach my spirit?

The wind rattles at the window,
there is a stirring abroad ...

God, or spirit, or presence,
how can I pass my spirit through you,
fuse myself into something new?

Like coffee, like smoke, I cry,
transmute my spirit too.

Commuter's lament

I am so tired by this life
that I would stretch myself out
on the pavement,
in the middle of the rush hour's drone,
and hum myself to sleep …

In my sleep I would dream
of my own sleeping:
how my snoring would rumble through
the pointless City
and flick off switches as it went
until everything was shut down
and people would file off home
to do something more useful instead –
face-painting, roller-skating, advanced gravy-making,
bed.

As I slept, a kindly old businessman –
who understood well the folly of things –
would softly slip a cheque for a million
in my top pocket,
and when I awoke I would away
to live next the sun by the beach
by the sea,
there to sell oranges, and tangerines,
and watch my children grow,
nut-brown, sun-ripe, free …

But how wide I dream!
I would not even *reach* sleep:
tutting commuters would tread on me,
scuff me, tramp, tramp, trampoline
(I would do the same myself).
No. I would bounce back up
before I had hummed two bars,
and march on, a tired chorus
in the endless song.

And when I got to the office,
smiling, I would apologise for running late
and quietly turn my computer on.

Spaces

Some days are just
empty spaces
to sit in or lie in
or snooze …

It's nice that way:
not every day
is an existential battle.
There is some slack
here and there,
time to take the air
or doze in it,
idly flick a page.

Does it matter
if a day goes to waste?
There are so many of them,
an almost endless supply …

The battle cry
can come another day.
This day's for doing nothing,
for existing as emptily,
as neutrally,
as a deckchair
or a bottle.

So I'll slip out of this day
like the shadows
lengthening in the garden,
leave it quietly
like the sun itself
which is going down
without fuss
behind a gradual gathering
of cloud.

Mark Hamilton

Springshine

It's a lazy daze
in the haze of the garden;
the sun, suddenly strong, pours in
like warmth filling up a bowl.
We loll in it gently,
let it lap at legs and arms.
What bliss is this
after six months of cold!
Air is light, and bright,
and floats in eddies
benign and kind.
Even, in this warmth,
we go barefoot for now,
padding in the kitchen
to make cold drinks
with clinks of ice and straws!

It will not last or hold
in these old northern climes
but for now one can believe
- if not too great a fool -
that life is deep-down good,
happy like a paddling pool.

Milk time

My son, how you suckle at the edge of sleep,
your quick life stilled beneath its slow dark charm;
all life is now the river from that teat
that leads you to the sea of sleep's deep calm.

You pull on that milk like the moon on the sea,
you are as natural as weather, as whole,
you're finished like adults can never be:
all that you do is the sum of your soul.

I think it's thought that splinters our being,
divides us into me, and many more –
pulls us from plenitude, kicks us, unseeing,
into a ragged, unconscious civil war.

But you – wrapped in peace on the rolling tide,
you're close-stitched in yourself as you're far, you're wide!

November ember

Dull afternoon sky
like a bruised fruit;
leaves peeling off the trees like
unplayed notes,
discarded sweepings
in a world's
tough gloom.

Cold air pushes round
carrying warnings of more
and other cold:
what could be, what will be,
what does, my friend …

At least it's warm inside – today.

What else may be may not be known,
not by you, not by the darkness
that steadily falls, wraps itself
round everything it finds
like a scarf full
of wide ironic
holes.

Graveside

"All right there Jase. How's it going?"
is my usual opening line.

It's usually cold, being late Feb,
with a wind worrying at the hedges.
I shuffle there, inspecting your grave,
the leaning headstone ("erected
by his family and many friends"),
the borderless edge which every year
I vow to sort and never do.

I don't know what to say next,
place the flowers, sniff the air,
fiddle in front of silence.

"You're not missing much Jase,"
is usually my next remark.

I like to think that under the ground
lies the huge wordless wisdom of the dead,
that you became safely part of.
Your life, cut short, briefly blazed,
then moved along. This year, year twenty one –
so your death is nearly equal with your life,
soon will overtake and endlessly outlast it.

I stay a while and tell you that I loved you,
my foster brother, cool and warm,
now far from the madding crowd
in this crowded plot, fuller year by year.

I looked for my soul

I looked for my soul in the shade of the trees
and listened for its note in the stir of a breeze;
I looked for my soul in summer's night sky
and caught at a tremor as a shadow swooped by.

I looked for my soul within my own poor frame
and squeezed for its essence in my own poor brain;
I looked for my soul just next to my heart
and traced with my tip where its course may start.

I looked for my soul in love's great *ahoy!*
and grasped for its secret in your fields of joy;
I looked for my soul by looking for yours
and craved for a oneness, a stillness, a pause ...

I looked for my soul, as for a holy visit,
but couldn't find, don't know what is it.

Snow fall

Snow falls overnight like love.
While no one looks, it is falling, falling …

It is a miracle in the morning:
All is transformed, touched from above.

Everything is changed – texture, light.
Children charge, heeding no warning,

They romp in this magical new dawning,
Swept up on a carpet of white.

Timeless, it at first may seem –
But world will tramp it in days like years,

Rains erode it with cold wet tears,
And it will vanish, like the traces of a dream.

Night song

My Cynthia dazzles in the deeps of night
and streams with stars of constellated light
along her lips and in her eyes.
My Cynthia strips from me the dimming husks
of weary stumbling through speculation's cusps
and lights me in fantastic skies.

She pulls the world in a surge of longing
up to the light where her glories are thronging
but fades before it can touch her.
She pulls me through hoops of twisted strangeness
and wakes me to cries of love and profaneness
which die in solitary rupture.

But *you*, Cynthia, waken only silence,
you rule the seas with the softest violence
of nocturnal starry calling.
But *you*, Cynthia, rise high beyond all sound
and vex me to pain that my achings resound
with nothing, but a soundless falling.

---

* Cynthia – Roman goddess of the moon

Days

There are days that are muffled,
when the sky is neutral
and leaves vacantly rustle.
There are times, when you sit
conversing in a crowded room,
I look at you dimly
and can turn a page unmoved.
There are days when I look
and a beauty does not scream out
at my weakening form;
when I look, and like you,
and warm to a peaceful glow.
Then agony is abated, and I move free,
and a tree is just a tree
and you seem what you are;
so that I wonder at my excesses,
and muse, and do not understand.

In such days, when the moon is not seen
and you are veiled in quietness,
a calmness caresses my mind
and spreads itself out through my frame
until a lost pain trembles
and I feel a weeping within.

Early morning

A dove or is it a pigeon coos in the early morning
feels so early in the early morning
the cars go by only one by one you can count them
coming like statements or is it questions
in the early morning
it is light so light in the early morning
long before six
why is it light so early in the early mornings
of summer
it is watery and pastel and newly forming
this curtain of light that has opened
across the sky – sigh –
a light has come on and you're awake
and nothing to do but get up
when in the week you crawl out of bed
like a snail with the alarm ...
Saturday it is and it's early
and you're up, coffee steams in the pot
and soon a cigarette will be lit and curling.
Small excitements, how old are you? (Forty-six)
What's to be done now, in the early morning?
Drink in this quietness, telly on low,
watch the early morning become not early
but just morning, heading even to afternoon;
suck perhaps sadly on your coffee spoon.

A swim at Foca

If my end came now
it would come well!

A swim in the Aegean sea,
glassy-cool then honey-warm,
cloudy-clear, scattered rich
with stones and shells
that lie like gifts
on the timeless sea floor.

Then Turkish *kahve*
in the breeze-blessed shade,
deep-earth black, silt
of the great land, strong
as an inverted sun; I praise it
with the lighting
of the fragrant leaf,
smoke fainting
in the burning air …

I wish my soul
would slip away now
up through these carob trees
with this bliss!

For is there anything more
to see or do,
after this?

Mark Hamilton works as a freelance copywriter. He has had a number of poems published in various poetry magazines and, in 2015, read at the Holloway Arts Festival in London. He also read poetry at Sanctum, a continuous public arts event in Bristol.

In Badock's Wood and Other Poems is his third poetry collection, and the first to be published in print. All three collections are available as eBooks.

Born in Bristol, Mark lives with his wife and their two children, just a short walk from Badock's Wood.